I0011315

The Bare Bones Book of Online Marketing:
Organic SEO, Google AdWords PPC, SEM & Social Media
For Business

Includes screenshots & examples

By J.T. Clark
(Author of "The Bare Bones Book of Screenwriting" and Founder of Clarkseo.com - with over 15 yrs. Experience Marketing Over 2,000 Websites.)

WBC Publishing
PO Box 874023
Vancouver, WA 98687
(P) 323.447.9676
info@clarkseo.com

First Edition

BISAC:
BUS090010 / BUS080000 / BUS043000

Paperback ISBN-13: 978-0-9795102-2-9
E-book ISBN-13: 978-0-9795102-6-7

Library of Congress Control Number (LCCN): 2014912397

Table of Contents

Chapter 1:
Understand the online marketing advantage and getting started…

We are in the digital age. Google, Yahoo, Bing and other search engines, email as well as smart phones, tablets, apps, laptops and computers are a foundation for the internet and the new form of how commerce is conducted worldwide. If you run a business, and want to sale your products and services, your livelihood now depends heavily on your website's strength, strategy and competency to gain exposure on the search engines, as much as brand, and offline efforts.

Just like an offline business, getting customers is quite a tough job. Though, plenty of methods of advertising and marketing are available that drive high-quality traffic, conversions depend solely on the interest of the customers and the way things are presented to them.

Traditional forms of marketing such as radio, television and print ads have been successful for many decades for a good reason: they reached a large number of potential customers in a short time period. The downside is that this form of "interruption" marketing also reaches many people who are not potential customers for a product or service. This can lead to low return on investment (ROI) and annoying cold call type of marketing.

With the advent of the internet and search engines and strategic marketing knowledge, there is a way to target only those customers who are actually interested in your product or service, quickly. Search engine marketing (SEM) has many advantages for a business that wants to broaden its reach by targeting the best potential online customers and gain quality leads. SEM is just one term and form of internet advertising. This book covers all aspects of online marketing for the novice to tech savvy web masters.

WHY ONLINE MARKETING WORKS

1) Online marketing works 24 hours a day. No matter when customers search the web, they will find marketing targeted at them.

2) Online Searchers are highly qualified prospects. Customers divide themselves into potential target groups based on what they choose to search for, rather than forcing the business to discover which individuals may be interested in a product.

3) Both small and large businesses can take advantage. While a business may not have the budget to compete in terms of expensive television advertising or large print ads, almost any business can afford to optimize a website for SEO content to attract visitors.

4) Immediate, measurable results. Results can be measured and tracked in real time, daily, monthly, annually, and adjusted to ensure a good return on advertising investment. But it needs maintaining.

5) Success is guaranteed. Unlike many marketing avenues such as placing an ad in a magazine, online marketing done well actually brings leads and the effects are long-lasting.

Search engine marketing can be the most cost-effective advertising a business ever uses. But it is constantly shifting. With the help of this book and some technical knowledge or an in-house webmaster, businesses can harness the power of the internet to drive customers to their websites quickly and raise profits immediately using the foundational "Bare Bones" online marketing techniques.

What is online marketing and why is so important for you and your business?

The internet changed the way businesses function, including how they generate brand awareness, leads and sales.

By now many businesses have heard of SEO - otherwise known as search engine optimization. If not, you'd better start paying attention because your financial future depends on it.

In the "good 'ol days" (before the millennium) consumers were conditioned to find services or products through magazines, yellow pages, word of mouth, newspaper, catalogs and so forth. Research depended heavily on physical books, libraries, etc. It required phone calls, gas money, time, energy, and frustration. As the internet grows, more and more consumers are unconsciously relying on search to find what they want – it's a natural evolution coinciding with the digital age and the explosive power of the internet.

As the baby boomer generation grows older, and the millennium generation takes the reigns, the percentage of internet savvy consumers infiltrates the marketplace and the technology to incorporate search expands continually and will for generations.

WHAT IS SEARCH?

"Search" is simple. Most people have heard "Google it." Since Google has positioned its brand alongside the development of internet growth and search technology it's synonymous with the word search – and blew Yahoo! Out of the water. The idea of the consumer simply typing in what they want and finding results has arrived… big time. And it continues to develop alongside other advancements such as GPS, and mobile phones, and devices like Google Goggles/Glasses – allowing interactive computing.

Why is search important to business? Because a business wants consumers to find them. And consumers want to find their target business accurately… and quickly. And with the evolving economy, technological revolution, short attention spans, "green" thinking and nearly every household owning a computer with internet access, search is the emerging pathway for consumers to find products and services in real time. Internet access is now subsidized for free or deeply discounted for low income families. To know SEO, you must understand the basics of a search engine. A search engine is not a directory. A directory is an organized hub with categories and listings within those categories. A search engine is a host to millions of websites archived by indexing them like a library. But there is no directory to find the books. You have to search by relevancy. To achieve relevancy and trust is the idea behind good online marketing. As of 2014, the top three search engines are Google, Yahoo! and BING (formally MSN.com)… in that order. Google owns an estimated 69% of the search market, while Yahoo! Owns an estimated 12%, Bing an estimated 14%, and the other minor search engines own the rest. It's a no brainer. You need to rank on Google.

Instead of using a search engine like a library to look up a specific book, a consumer uses a search tool to type keywords which brings up relevant search results based off how the search engine values the indexes. *The search term "dog leashes"* was typed into Google to get this set of mixed results below. The paid ads are on top and right. Shopping ads on right top. The organic ads cover ¾ the page.

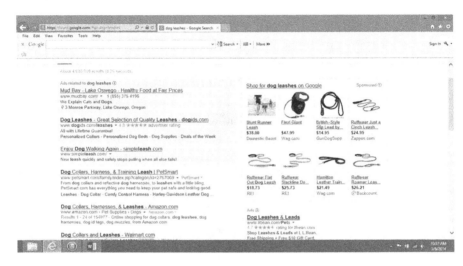

What paid and non-paid results are displayed is important to understanding search engine optimization. The displayed results are what the specific search engine deems most valuable based on several factors (those factors are the principal measuring points for SEO site positioning).

The results are pulled from the recorded content on your site called a cache. A cache is like a thumbprint of your website on the backend. When the search engine spiders crawl your content and HTML or website format files, they determine the rank and cache your page. If you make changes to your website, the cache will not change instantly, therefore the results will not change until the spiders re-crawl your pages. Spiders or robots are always crawling the web and your website for new data to index.

You can find the cached pages of your website by typing in

"site:www.yoursite.com" on a search engine search box.

The importance of the cache is high. If spiders don't like your web content, or find problems with your site, they consider it spam and will not cache the site which means you will not be displayed in search results, or removed completely.

LOCAL SEARCH

When doing searches for a local company product or service you may see a map with Google Places listings. These are local business map listings that will show close to your computer IP location. The major search engines have their own program you must submit your listing information to. Google's is called "Google Places" formally known as Google Maps. Below is a screenshot of a local search for Walmart:

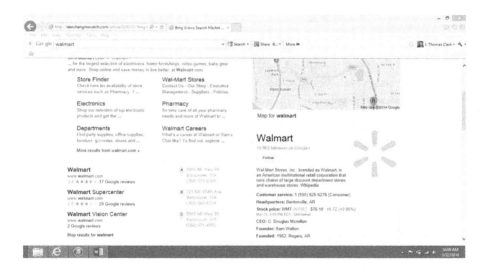

The above screenshot of a search for Walmart (the search was typed several miles from the IP location). A local search query brings up a map of the closest locations, and the Google Places listings on the left below organic listings.

Not all businesses benefit off local search, as many businesses are national or international. But a local market, hair stylist, tire shop, etc... can see some action off of local searches. It's hard to optimize local searches. The best method is to submit your site to Google Places, Yahoo Local and Bing Local. There are also companies that specialize in local search services.

Specific SEO/SEM factors will be explored later. For now, all you need to know is that the search engines judge your website and display content in many forms online based on your content and competition for top position for keywords or phrases in terms of relevancy, accuracy and dependability – according to each search engine's regulations.

The entire goal of SEO is to have your website display in the results of popular keywords and high volume search phrases that in turn bring high targeted traffic to your website for free. Sounds a lot better than mailing flyers out across town, or cold calls, doesn't it? SEO is a constant work in progress since algorithms are evolving and competition adapts to the SEO landscape, making for an interesting advertising channel constantly in motion.

The mechanics of valuing a website for ranking position is processed by what is known as an algorithm. **The algorithm** is a complex infrastructure of calculations designed to rate the value of websites according to searches. Search engines want the best algorithms to ensure the most relevant websites display on searches, because they want consumers to trust them. Search engines all have different experience, staff, technology and consumers, hence each search engine has a different algorithm. And these algorithms are updated frequently (which changes the search results).

So the study of SEO is also the study of the evolving algorithm.

In mathematics and computer science, an algorithm is a step-by-step procedure for calculations.

Now how does an algorithm process the information of your website and rank it? It uses a robot, or "spider." The spider is a robot that crawls the search engine and indexes the information found in the source code. Source code is the format the website was written in – it's language. To understand SEO, you must have a basic understanding of HTML language. If you do not know any HTML, I encourage you to stop now, Google HTML and do some tutorials for 15 minutes to get a grasp on what HTML code is. A spider crawls websites by crawling through links of other sites. Once it finds your site, it will stick around, collect information, and eventually index your website if it finds it valuable. A spider can also penalize your site for being considered spam, or move it down in priority based off competition and other factors.

Once your site is indexed, it means the impression of your websites (otherwise known as a cache) is cataloged by the search engine.

CACHE/INDEXED WEBSITE EXAMPLE

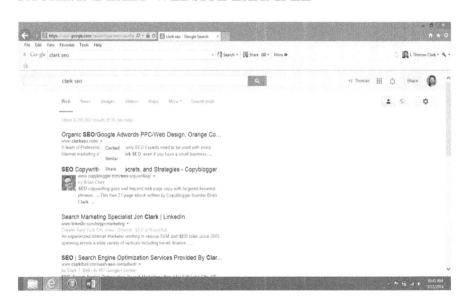

The cache version (catalogued in index) of your website pages and online content is in turn what yields traffic and results. Key searches pull indexed text and content from your site, which results in a display on the search engine. The display results list the title, and a description from the index able text.

When you click on the down arrow on the right of some search results (see cache image above) it creates a pop-down menu with cache. Select it and it takes you to the last updated/crawled version of your website and on the top will say:

*This is Google's cache of http://yoursite.com/. It is a snapshot of the page as it appeared on Mar 2, 2014 16:42:08 GMT. The current page could have changed in the meantime. Learn more Tip: To quickly find your search term on this page, press **Ctrl+F** or **⌘-F** (Mac) and use the find bar.*

The basic concept of SEO is to get your website(s) and social pages and local listings, etc... to appear on a search engine when the consumer searches for services or products similar to yours.

There are many ways to be "seen" or have your content rank.
- Organic
- Pay per click
- Local maps
- Social media sites
- Press releases
- Blogs/forums
- Shopping channels
- Direct traffic (from brand or referral)
- Link referral

The form by which consumers search for information is by keywords or key phrases (themes). For example, if you wanted to buy a camera you might type in "buy digital camera" or "digital camera for sale". Each search phrase would yield different results, and most likely different results on different search engines because the value of the website correlated with the two separate key phrases vary.

Why would the two results vary on one search engine from another? The algorithms are different, meaning the rules are different. On one search engine you have a little referee saying, "Goal." While on another search engine you could have a little referee saying, "Penalty!" It's tough to please each little referee, which is why most SEO is based off pleasing Google's little referee. Google hits the "G" spot.

Chapter 2:
Web Design Architecture
For Best Visibility in Search Engines

Smart SEO needs to start before your website is even up and running. First of all, the top search engines value the age of a registered domain name and hosted content. The longer your domain has been registered and content hosted on the domain, the less likely it is viewed as spam.

So if you know beforehand about your website, try and register a domain name and buy hosting and let it "simmer" for a year while developing the business off-line to gain trust. I suggest godaddy.com as it's very easy, but many options for domain and hosting are available.

Also, buy your registration and hosting in a 5 year block, this will gain trust as well because spammers tend to pay month to month and close the account when they are finished or have been caught.

Age is good/great/amazing. So good, in fact, that **it can be near impossible for sites five to ten years old to be outranked by newer sites.** Welcome to the reality of SEO… it is a giant gray area. But, diversity allows your site to compete online in other online marketing avenues while your organic SEO is building momentum.

CHOOSING A DOMAIN NAME

Uniqueness: You don't want consumers to get you and your competitors confused. Don't choose domain names that are plural, hyphenated or misspellings of your competitor's domains. But do try and use a keyword.

Pick a Dot-Com: If you want to build a successful brand website, use a dot-com as compared to a .org, .net, .biz, etc.

User friendliness: The easier to type, the more retention. You don't want an extremely long domain name, or hyphens, misspellings or you've just lost your brand. Keep the domain name short. Make your domain name catchy, relative, and unique. Your goal is to have people remember your name.

COPYRIGHT INFRINGEMENT

Before you register your domain name do some research on domain sites, and competitor trademarks.

Let us say you want the domain name
www.pigglywigglytoyboxcompany.com.

(Sorry if someone actually owns this.) Well, even if that domain name is available, there may be a piggly toy box trademark.

What this means is, if two years down the line, the company who did business as Piggly Toy Box before you did, has the legal right to the domain name or part of the domain, leaving you with two years of wasted branding and a domain name you will now forfeit the domains/websites.

Hyphens and Numbers: Use only as a last resort. Both numbers and hyphens are hard to remember, or confuse the consumer and the search engines.

Case Sensitive: Don't make your URL case sensitive.

UNDERSTANDING WEB SPIDERS

They don't call it "the web" for nothing.

When you look at the concept of the internet, it's a form of communication and connection between many sources in an infinite "web". The web contains websites. To reach to or to be reached from websites (a relationship), you need a web, or LINK so that a search spider (or robot) can crawl that line in the web and onto another website.

Each search engine has their own spiders, programmed to crawl the internet and websites.

Search spiders are usually crawling your files and pages in your root folders <u>every day</u>. When you make a change, the spider eventually finds it, and re-indexes the updated information which will reflect in the search engine results.

If you are creating a website from scratch, or thinking about starting an SEO campaign, you need to be aware of how web spiders crawls information on your site.

A spider moves through your site much like a human eye – from top-left-right-down – munching on information, indexing pages, and following links. One of the important things to remember, is that the most effective content and keywords need to be placed higher on the page/source code than the least important content.

As previously mentioned, Spiders or web crawlers index your web pages and determine the importance which helps you rank for key terms. Let us just say these little things are extremely important to your success, therefore you need to know how they interact with your website when they feed off it.

Use Visible Text

Spiders mainly process <u>visible text</u> in the source files (along with image files tagged, meta tags, links, and PDF files.) This means that flash files and images are not read by spiders. What does this mean? A website with nothing but flash, photos and videos may look amazing, but the spiders will pass you because they have nothing to feed on. Since they have nothing to feed on, you will not rank, you will not receive traffic, you will not generate sales. You will die. Not literally. But it will feel like death.

ALT TAGS: Optimizing an Image

You can embed within source code on images called "alt" tags or "title" tags. Written content should be in text and not written on image files like a picture/graphic.

In your website backend you can tag an image or flash with an "alt" tag like this:

<img src="kidswimming.jpg" alt="Kid Swimming">

- which when scrolled over on the webpage will expose a small pop up with the text contained inside. Using alt tags are important for having your photos appear on image results and social media marketing.

Frames and Flash: <u>not</u> SEO friendly

For the non-tech reading this you are asking what is a frame? A frame is a frame of one webpage embedded into another page. It appears as part of the page, but a separate entity programmed in the code.

Think of a frame as a picture frame on a wall. Frames are two different web pages displayed on one screen. It may appear to be aesthetically pleasing to a visitor, but spiders treat frames and i-frames separately. As for flash videos and media, just know that flash and media carry very limited weight for SEO rankings. Use text where possible.

Static URL's

Spiders can only understand a permanent, static URL that is not constantly shifting so the spiders know where to go to find information.

JavaScript: <u>not</u> SEO friendly

Spiders cannot read JavaScript. Any link or text portrayed by JavaScript will not be indexed. Stop using JavaScript for navigation, and stick with HTML text links.

Use a Site map

A site map is good for spiders, organization and visitor retention. For new sites they are critical. It can take search engines months to crawl a new site pages. Adding a sitemap can speed up the process, by allowing a pathway for search spiders to enter all your web pages, and determining index and authority.

Create a site map with links to every page on it. Put the link to the site map on the bottom of every page. This will help spiders find all the pages on your site because spiders follow links. Each page of your website is indexed differently, at different times, because spiders index your pages, not all your pages under the domain at the same time.

Using a sitemap ensures links point to your website from other internal pages.

A HTML based sitemap is a good idea, but XML sitemap is not needed, but also not a bad idea. I've found no proof a XML helps SEO but I do not discredit it either.

Keyword content & placement

Your keyword strategy is key to SEO. Why? Because people search by keywords and key phrases, and they almost never search for your company name unless your company name is a household brand name or referral.

Question: How does a spider crawl your website?

Answer: Like a human reading a book. Left to right. Top to bottom.

The closer to the **top left** your keywords are, the more weight the search engine gives them because it is more important. The best strategy for success is to place you most important keywords or phrases higher up on the page and top left. This is true also for meta title, description and meta keywords. (We'll discuss meta tags later.)

Keyword selection and placement is only one factor in ranking. But it is essential.

First you have to know what your keywords are:

So. Logistically, the first step of SEO is choosing your keywords and finding the words that you can rank for with the highest volume and reasonable competition.

Google Insights is a tool which allows you to compare the volume of searches by comparing phrases. It shows you which countries and territories have the highest volume of key phrases.

Go to: Google Insights, or Google Trends, or keywordspy.com.

1) **Selection:** Determine what keywords and phrases your customers are using to find your products. Type in the keywords and see if your competitors pop up. If so, then these are the phrases you will be competing for.

2) *Example: you sell Dolls but you are not Mattel. Here are a group of terms you would want to rank for: buy dolls, dolls for sale, shop for dolls, cheap dolls, affordable children's dolls, dolls for kids, buy dolls online, etc...*

3) **Be realistic.** If you own a car lot, you will not be able to rank for "cars for sale" or "buy cars". You have too much competition.

Besides common sense, the way to roughly gauge your competition level is to see how many sites are competing for a particular search term. You can locate the number on a search engine as seen below for search "dog leashes" on Google – over 4 million pages competing for the term. (Top in light gray.)

The total# is not the total number of sites competing with you, but rather the total number of sites that display under the particular search term. The more sites that display, the more sites you must compete against to gain the ranking that people will see. My personal suggestion to newbies is to try and rank for terms that have under 1 million. You may get lucky here and there, but competing against 2+ million listings is no easy task.

4) **Once you've selected your handful of keywords** and phrases you want to rank for, you need to optimize your website for those words. Sprinkle your keywords in your meta tags, headers, and on-page content, links and alt tags.

KEYWORD DENSITY (on-page factor)

Keyword density is the relation between the percentages of keywords compared to the entire percentage of words on the web page. This was about the only way to rank in the past, before search engines became sophisticated and incorporated all aspects of image, video, blogs, PPC, social media, etc.

You don't want to oversaturate your on-page content with too many keywords – which is referred to as "stuffing". Stuffing is a "no-no" in the SEO world, and can get you banned from search engines. You want your keyword density levels to hover around 5% – 15%. When researching your key terms, run a density check on your competitor's sites.

The way to measure keyword densities is to use an SEO tool. There are many freebies on the internet, just Google, "keyword density tools". IBP is SEO software with many features including density tools. If you are serious about SEO, it is worth the few hundred dollars a year.

LONG-TAIL KEYWORDS (psychology of searchers)

When a keyword or key terms are tough to compete against, many alternative organic keyword opportunities can be available by optimizing for keyword combinations with 3-5 words, with less competition. More than 60% of most organic search traffic comes from long-tail keyword search. Don't try and climb the biggest mountain first. It takes time. Consumers type in abstract keyword combinations to get results.

META TAGS

Meta tags are hidden tags in your source files (HTML, PHP, etc.) or on your blogs backend platform CMS – content management system - that relate to keywords and help search engines determine what your site is about. Meta tags are VERY IMPORTANT. They are a staple of organic SEO success.

Meta Titles:

Your meta title is what appears as ad copy headline in the browser so a page can attract a click:

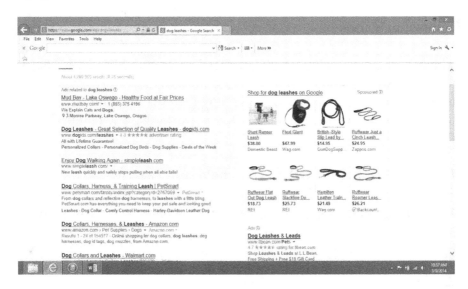

If you know HTML the title tag is constructed as below:

<title>Dog Leashes</title>

All search engines only display a certain amount of characters in your title. A good rule to go by is to use 55 characters otherwise the title gets cut off. You want to use your best keywords in the title that you will repeat in your on-page content and links. A title should contain keywords but also be enticing for visitors to click on. Think of it as a sales ad.

Meta Descriptions:

The meta description tag is an important HTML tag you embed under the title tag. Search engines rely heavily on description tags to rank websites. Many times, you will see the description display on search results like this:

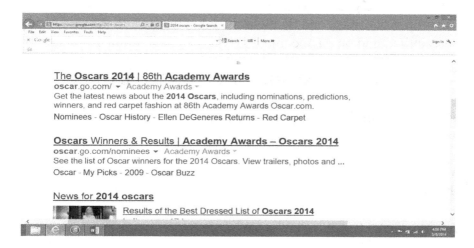

You want to keep the character count to around 250 characters. Use your most important words first. Here is how the HTML tag is written:

<meta name="description" content="Get the latest news about the 2014 Oscars....">

Meta Keyword Tag:

The meta keyword tag is controversial. Many claim it is not worth a thing, and others claim that it is magic. It probably falls somewhere in between worthless and helpful, but it's importance is insignificant when compared to the title, description or on-page content.

The meta keywords tag is invisible like all meta tags. It only appears in source code read by spiders, and is coded like this:

<meta name="keywords" content="keyword 1, keyword 2, keyword 3, etc"

Just make sure you use your most important keywords first, use proper densities, and tie these meta keywords into the title, description, and on page content. My advice, use about 10 terms.

USE DIFFERENT META TAGS ON EACH PAGE!!!

Using the same meta tags on every page is duplicate content, to be avoided.

You want each page to focus on ranking for specific terms and themes.

For example, if you owned a pet shop Miami, your main page would probably be optimized for "pet shop in Miami" or "Miami pet shops". But you would have pages that link off into other categories that get narrower and narrower. One category page may be all about dogs, therefore optimize it for related terms. Another page may be related to cats, so optimize that for related terms. Keyword stemming is the term for branching a main theme into smaller themes/pages. This is SEO friendly navigation, linking and structure.

Elements to Optimize with your Keywords:

1. Title tag:

The most important tag. 55 characters.

2. Meta descriptions

Keep under 265 characters. Don't repeat words too often. Write a clear sentence. Consumers will see this in the search results sometimes.

3. Meta keywords

Utilize the meta keyword tag for misspellings, and obscure phrases. Don't stuff keywords, and keep the tag to about 265 characters.

4. On-page textual content

Includes written text, alt tags and the phrases within the link text. Don't oversaturate keywords. 1-3 themes per page.

5. Major headings

Header tags start with <h1>text goes here</h1> and can be implemented up to <h6> - the least important heading tag. Using a <h1> tag is important, the rest are not so much. Make sure the <h1> tag contains your keywords from your title, description and on page phrases. </h1>

6. Anchor text

When linking to other pages, other websites, use anchor text containing your keywords.

Chapter 3:
Diverse Link Building

Links, or *hyperlinks* simply link a visitor from one web page to another by clicking and transferring to another URL. Usually they say "click here." Everyone who uses the internet clicks on links. They are usually embedded in text or displayed as an image advertisement. They default to appear in blue font. Links can direct visitors around your website or take them to sites away from your website. Don't hide links with the background color as this could lead to a penalty.

LINK BUILDING

Links play important roles in all aspects of online marketing and SEO by giving your site, blog, image strength ("link juice") and thematic relevancy & rank position. Building links is essential for site strength, traffic, ranking, branding and sales. Ideally you want one way links (links pointing to your site) but swapping links can be of value as well. Best case scenario for your links is to have your best keywords and phrases as anchor text (keyword in link).

ANCHOR TEXT (keyword inside a link)

Anchor text is a major component to good ranking.
Anchor text is the text contained within an actual link. Unskilled webmasters use words like "click here" or "click to buy" within their links for consumers to click on, which brings them to a new page.

Here is how anchor text is formatted using HTML:

<a href="http://www.anothersite.com">click here!</a>

By clicking on "click here" in the link text displayed on the website, a visitor is directed to a new page. Well, **the words "click here" is the anchor text.** Now, "click here" may be useful to let a consumer know to click there, but it's not a useful term to show spiders what key terms are relevant for your consumers.

If you use the anchor text "find shoes"… then you will gain "link juice" and show the algorithm that your webpage is important for the term "find shoes". Anchor text and keywords are the foundations for keyword ranking and positioning organically. Now, the more times you have anchor text "find shoes" on your own web pages, in directory listings, or pages throughout the internet linking to a specific URL, the more relevancy you will have for the search term "find shoes". All search engines have their own rules for link density and stuffing.

OUTGOING LINKS (linking out to other websites)

Outgoing links are links that point out from the page that the link is on. An outgoing link can link away from your internal page on your own site or a completely different website. Whenever you link out, you are giving power to the page you link to. Linking is healthy internally, but linking out too much weakens your site unless that site also links back to you with the same thematic content as your site. That is called link reciprocity. Outgoing links are not all bad. The search engines will actually upgrade your authority if you link out to a few high authority sites with similar themes.

INCOMING LINKS (links coming into your site from another)

Incoming links are links pointing toward a page on your site. These are also called backlinks. Incoming links are very important to your SEO strategy. Links coming into your site give your site strength, as long as the page linking to yours is not spam, and the related website content is thematically similar. For best results, diversity is key. Links from a variety of sources creates trust.

INTERNAL LINKING (linking within your own site)

To start your link campaign is to create an internal linking strategy to give power to your pages to rank for specific searches. You want anchor text with keywords to point to certain pages to rank for the desired term. So if you want to rank for "Boston ice cream shop" make sure you have those words in your links on most of your pages pointing to your homepage. Remember, each time you link out, you give away power. Linking back to your homepage from other pages within the same URL gives strength back to the homepage. It's called "link juice" and the power of it passes from page to page. Like sucking gas from a car, a link sucks juice from that page and gives it t the page it links to.

NO FOLLOW TAGS (preserving your link juice)

Many times you will use links on your site which you want visitors to follow, but they aren't linked to important pages for ranking. Examples could be your contact page, or privacy policy page. You can put a no follow tag on your link so that spiders don't follow the link, and save the link juice for the page instead of giving the power to a page that receives little or nor traffic from organic rankings.

Here's how:

<a href="www.yoursite.com" rel="nofollow">click here</a>

LINK RECIPROCITY (trading links aka link exchange)

Also known as "swapping links" or "exchanging links" or "link campaign". Remember, when you give another site a link, you give power away. So you better get something in return. A link back to you from their website. But be careful. Is it a fair trade or are you getting screwed?

You must research and determine if the site that links back to you has similar content as you. If it doesn't, it hurts you. You also must determine what the page rank (PR) value of the site is that wants to link to you. If the page rank is low, then the link is worthless. Their site is weak. If their site has a grey bar in the Google PR tool it means it's new or penalized and weak – not worth trading.

Google seems to be cracking down on this, so it's not the best strategy. Balance is key.

Professional SEO campaigns depend on several factors. Keyword selection is important, but link building, and diversity of links is just as, if not more important - but they need to be stitched together. SEO experts analyze in depth your website, to determine the best course of action if you lack the skills.

A custom backlink program is needed to establish authority in the online market. With Panda and Penguin and Hummingbird and Frog (ok I made that up) algorithms from Google, SEO content and on and off page website factors impact rankings in a new way.

The wrong link strategy can make you lose rankings.

Website authority does not just happen. It takes time, and SEO experts. One good link is better than 1,000 worthless links. Google and other search engines love links - the right links - as they equate it to a vote, or popularity contest, which makes authority. Unethical SEO is all about the short term, quickie link building campaign. Not wise. Many websites lose rankings, sometimes forever. So, experience counts.

Good forms of link building
- Blog posts
- Forum posts
- Press releases
- Social media links
- Local search links
- Local business listings
- Directories (niche or business)

Bad linking methods
- Too many links on one page
- Too many outgoing links
- No site map
- Automatic paid link schemes
- Link farms
- Links on non-relevant websites
- Links on penalized websites

Directories

The quickest way to build trust is to get high quality links on the internet's best and oldest directories and variety.

This is a list of web directories & reviewed web guides:

Business.com

DMOZ.org - also known as the Open Directory Project (Google's own directory) - provides free listings, but it may take a while to get your site listed. If you get listed at all.

Gimpsy

GoGuides

JoeANT

Lycos Directory

Skaffe

Uncover the Net

Wow Directory

Yahoo Directory

Toporangecountybusinessdirectory.com

Chapter 4:
How to analyze your competition

HOW TO CHECK (PR) PAGE RANK VALUE

Google has this thing called Page Rank (AKA "PR"). It is Google's measurement of how valuable a webpage is according to its rules. The scale is 0 - 10, with 10 being the highest. New sites will have a grey bar for months before a 0. Your site will not improve its page rank until Google does a major re-crawl of all the sites, which happens about every 3 – 6 months (more later). One way to know instantly what a webpages PR value is, is to download the Google toolbar.

Google Toolbar: http://toolbar.google.com/T4/index_pack_xp.html

The tool will display across your browser with many tool options. One tool is the page rank tool bar, which displays a horizontal green bar displaying the strength of a site. Whenever you visit a site, the site's page rank value is shown. This allows you to gauge the competition and monitor your own sites. See top middle of screenshot below: Location of the PR bar.

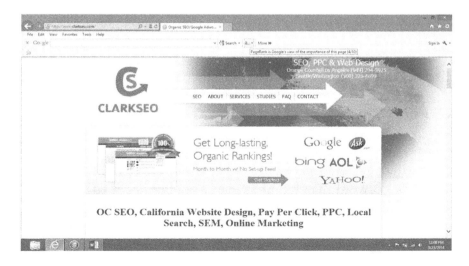

To give you an idea of how the scale works, most sites will have a PR value of 1 – 3. Large corporate sites can have a PR value of 5 – 7, while there are very few sites with an 8 – 10 PR value.

The higher the PR value, the more authority Google determines the site has, therefore, the more strength the site has. Therefore the more strength the link has when linking back to your site.

Obviously, you want links to your site from strong sites with high PR value WITH similar thematic content pertaining to your own site. What you don't want is links to your site from low value (grey – 0 PR) sites. And you don't want sites linking to you (besides directories) that have unrelated thematic keyword content). For example, it is not good to have a link from a soda company linking to a pet food website. It's not logically related, and the search engines may penalize or de-mote your site.

How to analyze competitor links:

You can go to Alexa.com and find out what sites link into a website. Also site traffic stats. They offer free and paid services.

Keywords

If you want to be a sneaky keyword spy there's a site for that. www.keywordspy.com. You can also do searches through the Google AdWords keyword search tool or search engines for related keywords. Look at source code for meta tags. Analyze their on-page text content. Do the above and you can determine a competitor's main driving themes and keywords they are targeting.

Domains

Want to find out who owns a domain and for how long? No problem. Go to Google.com and type - who is "domain name" – and include the quotes. A list of information data based sites populate with info on the domain holder, registration date, contact info, etc. Sometimes the info is hidden by a special registration or by parent company or hosting company.

Sneak a peak at your competitor caches:

Want to find indexed pages of your competitor's website or blog?

Type **site:domain.com** into the search engine.

You can easily search your industry online and find images, videos, social media sites, press releases, blogs, etc. Put in elbow grease on your spy work.

Use SEO software

IBP pro and other SEO software lets you analyze website rankings, backlinks and criteria compared to your site.

The Way Back Machine

There is a website that collects old caches of sites so that a nosey marketer can look into the past to see versions of a website years or decades back in time, older designs and indexed copies. http:// archive.org/web/

Chapter 5
Organic SEO (search engine optimization)

Search engines are not directories. Directories are not search engines.

A search engine is a library of websites in an infinite box. To find what you want, you need to search descriptive words into a box. Having your website appear when a consumer type in those words in the box, is what online marketing is – leading to lead generating, sales and revenue.

Wikipedia Defines SEO:

Search engine optimization (SEO) is the process of improving the volume and quality of traffic to a web site from search engines via "natural" ("organic" or "algorithmic") search results for targeted keywords. Usually, the earlier a site is presented in the search results or the higher it "ranks", the more searchers will visit that site. SEO can also target different kinds of searches, including image search, local search, and industry-specific vertical search engines.

MAIN FACTORS FOR POSITIONING

Algorithms contain rules for thousands of variables, but there is a basic set of rules that any SEO specialist must understand in order to begin an SEO campaign, or at least understand where to start, how to start, and when to start.

The basic following factors are important for top rankings and high traffic:

1) Age of domain:
2) Keyword based content
3) Organization
4) PR value (Google only)
5) Traffic/Popularity
6) Diversity, authority of links
7) Website architecture
8) Number of pages per visitor
9) Time spent on site
10) Social media factors

A snapshot of the search industry: Google is here to stay always keeping around a 70% or higher share of the market. Yahoo! and Bing are strong but together can't take down G. AOL and Dogpile, Excite are considered minor search engines because they only account for 2% or less of the market combined.

Google.com is a Web search engine owned by Google, Inc., and it is the most used search engine on the Web. Google receives several hundred million queries each day through its various services. Like the internet and computers, Google changed the world. Embrace it. **Google is not a trend – it's a platform.**

The domain google.com attracted over 190 million unique visitors a month in 2013.

PageRank

Google's algorithm uses a patented system called PageRank to help rank web pages that match a given search string. The PageRank algorithm computes a recursive score for web pages. The PageRank derives from human-generated links, and correlates well with human concepts of importance.

The exact percentage of the total of web pages that Google indexes are not known, as it is very hard to actually calculate it. Previous keyword-based methods of ranking search results, used by many search engines that were once more popular than Google, would rank pages by how often the search terms occurred in the page, or how strongly associated the search terms were within each resulting page. In addition to PageRank, Google also uses thousands of hidden and patented criteria for determining the ranking of pages.

Search results

Google's search engine takes "snapshots" of PDFs, images, web pages, blogs, profiles, Word documents, Excel spreadsheets, Flash SWF, plain text files and much more. Except in the case of text and SWF files, the cached version is a conversion to (X) HTML, allowing those without the correct viewer applications to read the file.

Users can customize the search engine, by setting a default language, using the "SafeSearch" filtering technology and set the number of results shown on each page. Google has been criticized for placing long-term cookies on users' machines to store these preferences, a tactic which also enables them to track a user's search terms and retain the data for more than a year. Probably forever.

Google optimization

Since Google is the most popular search engine, many webmasters are wise to influence their website's Google rankings. An industry of consultants has arisen to help sites raise their rankings on Google, Yahoo!, Bing and on other search engines. This field, called search engine optimization/SEO, attempts to discern patterns in search engine listings, and then develop a method for improving rankings & generating leads.

Some SEO firms have attempted to inflate specific Google rankings by various artifices, and thereby draw more searchers to their client's website. Google's big challenges have been to lessen attempts by reducing the ranking of websites.

Search engine optimization encompasses both "on page" factors (like body copy, title tags, H1 heading tags and image alt attributes) and Off Page Optimization factors (Like anchor text, social media, linking). The general idea is to affect Google's relevance algorithm by incorporating the keywords being targeted in various places "on page", in particular the title tag and the body copy (note: the higher up in the page, the better its keyword prominence and thus the ranking). Too many occurrences of the keyword, however, cause the page to look suspect to Google's spam checking algorithms. (See *keyword stuffing*.)

Getting listed

To get indexed by search engines you need to get listed by them, which is determined by spiders that crawl the net. Spiders help your site or ruin your life by removing your website if it is not in compliance or helping you get more sales and rankings if your SEO is great.

To get indexed, you can submit your new URL/site to each search engine, hire a service, or simply get backlinks and eventually the spiders will find your new URL and index it if it is not spam.

Here are the advantages of quality indexing:

- You will get indexed to googles directory as it will follow to your site/blog from the link - this is weighed more.

- You get automatically linked once when a google robot follows the link - no desperate wait.

- Guarantee traffic in less time.

Google sandbox

Just because you get indexed by Google and other search engines does not mean your site will rank. In fact, the opposite, it will suck for a while. Google and engines put new sites on a leash for year 1. 5 year old sites preform best. Time is a factor of trust, trust is a factor of rankings. Momentum and trust are vital.

A popular method is to go to a domain auction and buy a 5 year old domain with your company or keyword in it. You'll be off to a good start.

New domains retain ranking restrictions which are loosened by SEO, but it takes time. Meanwhile, pay per click is instant.

Search engine updates

The world of search changes daily, so do rankings sometimes. It is volatile with competition, economy, and to make it more interesting, the search engines update their criteria for rankings VERY frequently. Actually there's an update on Google search engine almost daily, probably several small ones a day. These updates can increase your PR value and rankings.

Google and all search engines have their own similar algorithm, or criteria to place for keywords or terms – and all of them frequently update their criteria. Almost every quarter. Google announces their updates and has silly names for them like Panda, Penguin, Hummingbird, etc. These updates sound sweet, but they can rip you website limb from limb – metaphorically speaking.

This is where organic SEO comes into play. Everything is constantly changing, so your SEO (or you) need to constantly be up with the times or you can lose it all.

Each update is designed to implement new filters and rules to rank well and to weed out spam.

The conspiracy theorist in me thinks the search engines update the criteria so often so businesses have to rely on PPC/pay per click marketing alongside their organic SEO... as it is always in the air, up and down, in and out, advancing, declining. Your rankings have a life of their own. It's important to monitor your rankings with software like IBP or others. If you see a decline on an important keyword, you know what to focus on.

Example of a small Google update: Hummingbird

What type of "new" search activity does Hummingbird help?

"Conversational search" is one of the biggest examples Google gave. People, when speaking searches, may find it more useful to have a conversation. In particular, Google said that Hummingbird is paying more attention to each word in a query, ensuring that the whole query — the whole sentence or conversation or meaning — is taken into account, rather than particular words. The goal is that pages matching the meaning rank higher.

Branding and SEO

Your company branding is your most important business asset because your brand image becomes associated in the consumer's mind with a level of credibility, reliability, quality and satisfaction.

Your brand is a complex set of meanings and associations that motivate purchasing decisions and encourage customer loyalty.

Your brand takes on an identity that makes you unique by distinguishing and differentiating your company and its products and services and setting you apart from your competition in a crowded marketplace.

*Increase brand awareness and recognition for your products and services in order to increase online sales and trust for the future.

But regardless of how good your website looks, how good your brand is, and how good your product/service is, you still need to reach an audience. SEO helps your website reach your buyers and increase leads and sales.

So use your brand in your title, description, and use it in body text on pages. Also link using your brand name as anchor text.

REPUTATION MANAGEMENT

You've worked so hard or paid so much to that SEO company, and now there are unsatisfied customers out there... and they have the nerve to write a negative review! That will stay on the web... forever... and ever... and ever... no, really – it's there for good.

Trying to remove it is like trying find one grain of sand hidden on a beach. Once something goes out into the internet, it rarely returns.

It's not easy to eliminate negative content/reviews from websites being crawled by search engines and SEO'd on Google, Yahoo!, Bing.

Why do You Need Online Reputation Management?

So your company does not lose trust and sales in the untamable, aggressive online world.

You need advanced SEO strategies to improve positive mentions of your company resulting in lowering the placement of negative mentions to positions where most consumers will never see them.

Don't let website competitors or online enemies take your reputation down the toilet. Let a pro help your website and business regain it's rankings and excellent ratings.

All it takes is one jerk to ruin what you've built a lifetime to achieve. The internet can make or break your sales and leads online. And give you anxiety attacks.

Life isn't fair, but Clark SEO Consulting (www.clarkseo.com) or another SEO can regain balance and get more trust on your side so that when customers do search for your small business, they don't come across bad reviews and slanderous commentary about your products or services.

A seasoned SEO can push down negative reviews to pages further back, leaving your brand and site at the forefront.

Chapter 6:
Google AdWords Pay Per Click Advertising (PPC)

Setting up a Google AdWords account is simple. Go to Google AdWords sign up page and sign up.

Site: **adwords.google.com**

Running a successful AdWords campaign... <u>not</u> so easy.

AdWords is Google's main platform for advertising and main source of revenue ($32.2 billion in 2013). AdWords offers pay-per-click (PPC) advertising, and site-targeted advertising for both text and banner ads.

The AdWords program includes local, national, and international distribution. Google's text advertisements are short, consisting of one title line and two content text lines. Image ads can be one of several different Interactive Advertising Bureau (IAB) standard sizes.

AdWords is simply a bidding platform for businesses to compete online for keywords. Other search engines have their own paid platforms, but to keep it simple, we'll stick with speaking about AdWords as it is the most popular.

Google's AdWords division is based in Ann Arbor, Michigan, the company's third-largest facility behind its Mountain View, California, headquarters and New York City office.

Advertisers specify the words that should trigger their ads and the maximum amount they are willing to pay per click. When a user searches Google's search engine on www.google.com (or the relevant local/national google server (e.g. www.google.ca for Canada), ads for relevant words are shown as **"sponsored ads"** on the top and right of the screen, along with organic listings, map listings, shopping listings, image listings.

The pecking ordering of the paid listings depends on other advertisers' bids (PPC) and the "quality score" of all ads shown for a given search account.

The **quality score** is calculated by click-through rates and the relevance of an advertiser's ad text and keywords. The quality score is also used by Google to set the minimum bids for an advertiser's keywords. The exact formula is confidential to Google.

I highly recommend newbies to select "search only" when setting up a new campaign, and opt out of the partner and content networks. These can waste money to the novice. Search only will allow your ad impressions (appearances) only on Google search engine – prime online real estate space.

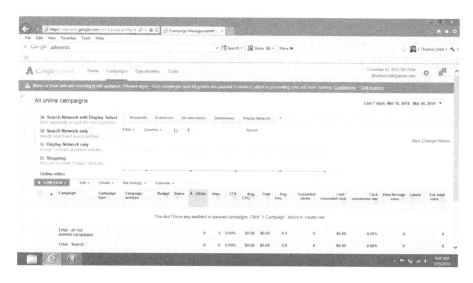

You can select the geo locations in which you want your ads to appear so you don't pay for clicks in areas you don't sell to. This can be broken down into country, states, counties, cities, towns.

Your ads will automatically be eligible for impressions on computers, laptops, and smart devices.

You can also adjust the mobile ad price and Minimize price per click under settings. If your product would not be suitable for mobile searches, then decrease amount on mobile ads you are willing to spend per click.

Keyword Match Types

Most non tech savvy business owners are already scratching their heads. Keep scratching, as things get complicated. You can select keywords to bid on, but there are 3 ways to set your keywords or phrases, when setting up your AdWords campaign.

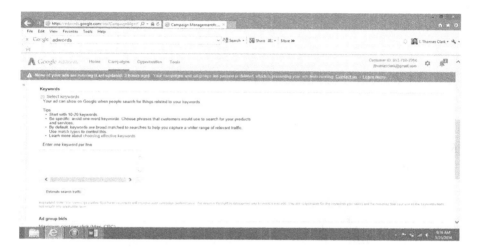

1. EXACT MATCH: [keyword]. Your ad only appears if it meets the bid requirement and a consumer searches the exact phrase. This could create low traffic, but high quality as your ad only appears when the exact word(s) are typed into the search engines like Google, Yahoo, Bing, etc.

2. PHRASE MATCH: "keyword". The ad only appears on phrase searches such as Portland "SEO and web design" services. The phrase between the brackets is the phrase match allowing the ad to appear on searches with words in front or at the end of the phrase. This is slightly tighter targeting as you know the click came from a search containing the phrase.

3. BROAD MATCH: keyword. The ad will appear when a consumer types the keyword(s) along with any other words before, in the middle, or after the keyword. Obviously, this is not as targeted and can cost tons of lost clicks and money.

AD COPY

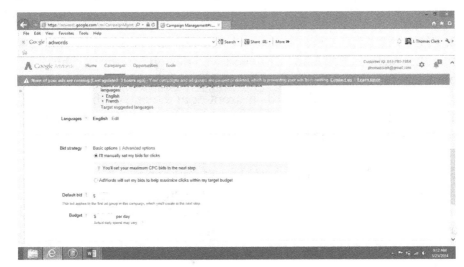

Keep it simple. Use relevant keywords. AdWords <u>does not</u> allow your phone number on the ad itself. And you can be infringing if you put your competitor's trade name within your advert. You only have a headline, 2 body lines, and a domain.

Setting CPC limits or automatic: When you set up a campaign, one of the steps is choosing to let Google determine the cost per click letting you create a ceiling, or limit per click. I suggest setting limits, as, well, do you really want to drive a car without steering? The AdSense system will gobble your money up in a split second if you let the system run on auto-pilot.

During the set-up menu you can choose to let Google run a budget for you (no thanks) or set a CPC (cost per click) limit. Most industries are around $1-$5/click, but some are as high as $20-$80/click. Do your research and testing and set a max. cost per click that gets you a low cost per click and decent position on Google. Aim for position 1-3, but having PPC ads on page 2,3,4,5 etc. of a search engine isn't a bad thing either as consumers search that deep.

AdWords promo codes

Google should give you a $75 or $100 promo code for a new account. Ask your AdWords rep if you don't see one. Don't waste your time searching Google for promo codes and trying them. It won't work. And if you try and open up several accounts, they can close them down. Trust me...

Also, if you keep paying for clicks Google sends you promo codes as a bone once in a while. But not often. Maybe once a year.

Split testing ads

All ads are not created equal. It is best to test 2-4 ads, study them for a week or two, then determine which ads have the highest ranking with the lowest cost. Pause the other ads, and create more to split test, equaling the best adverts with best ROI & cheapest cost per click.

WARNING! Google Content/Display Network

Another fork in the road decision while setting up campaign is choosing to allow your ads to run on Google search, Google partners, or the above plus the content/display network of sites containing AdSense creating junk clicks, fraud, waste.

Careful of the content/display network. Opting into the content network is like gambling. Its content sites are blogs or forums or spam sites that put AdSense code in their sites to support AdWords ads (what you are paying for).

Many times the sites are junk/spam or there can be **click fraud where <u>robots</u> or <u>persons</u> click on ads for a percentage of profit.**

The content network doesn't work well for many businesses.

AdWords can be complex for beginners

Google AdWords has gotten feature rich and complicated in the past few years. 50% of AdWords users give up managing their own campaigns and turn it over to a professional, which to a wise business is the best strategy. *Use a pro if your business needs Google AdWords management or set-up.*

Don't Obsess with the Competition

Focus on your target market and writing effective ad copy that gets a high click thru rate, driving down the cost per click from internet traffic. You can use free tools like Keyword Spy to see estimated costs per click on your keywords, and volume. Ensure to select target areas if you service or product is limited to a certain region, city, county, state or nation. Clark SEO can help with all the headaches and target customers in a niche market/space serving a single zip code or a worldwide campaign, eliminating bad markets and increasing focus on highest earning markets.

The #1 Spot Isn't Always the Best: "Plan B" Can Win

Everyone wants #1 spots - but does it make sense to your website and budget? If so, go for it - it'll cost you. But if you have a competitive online market-which nowadays every market is packed-then you can proceed with a cheaper pay per click campaign strategy and either aim for position 2-8 and still be on page 1, sometimes page 2. Your cost per click lowers, and impressions go up. Not everyone clicks or trust the first PPC ad on page one. For organic SEO, the opposite is the case – SEO firms want get you #1, page 1 positions for best ROI.

Chapter 7:
Mistakes and Google Penalty (negative SEO)

Don't be a naïve or naughty web marketer. Like Uncle Sam or Johnny Law, the search engines, especially Google will find you (and beat you madly).

Mistakes or short-cuts can lead to a website's permanent removal from the search engines, a deleted AdWords account, or a 6 month, 3 month, or eternal penalty.

Penalties can arise out of evil SEO or undereducated SEO's. They can be put on a website for on or off page factors, temporarily, or permanently by either robots or humans.

KEYWORD STUFFING (repetitive words)

Keyword stuffing is considered to be an unethical search engine optimization (SEO) technique. Keyword stuffing occurs when a web page is loaded with keywords in the meta tags or in content. The repetition of words in meta keyword tags may explain why many search engines no longer use these tags.

Keyword stuffing had been used in the past to obtain maximum search engine ranking and visibility for particular phrases. This method is completely outdated and adds no value to rankings today. In particular, Google no longer gives good rankings to pages employing this technique.

INVISIBLE TEXT (hide it, they will find it)

Hiding text from the visitor is done in many different ways. Text colored to blend with the background, CSS "Z" positioning to place text "behind" an image — and therefore out of view of the visitor — and CSS absolute positioning to have the text positioned far from the page center are all common techniques. As of 2005, some of these invisible text techniques can be detected by major search engines. "Noscript" tags are another way to place hidden content within a page.

While they are a valid optimization method for displaying an alternative representation of scripted content, they may be abused, since search engines may index content that is invisible to most visitors.

Inserted text sometimes includes words that are frequently searched (such as "sex"), even if those terms bear little connection to the content of a page, in order to attract traffic to advert-driven pages.

What is "hidden text?" It sounds so naughty. And it is. It's very very bad SEO.

Hidden text is textual content which your visitors cannot see, but which is still readable by the search engines. The idea is to load a web page with keywords and keyword phrases that would be unsightly to visitors but that would improve the page's rankings in the search engine results, and to do so without letting your visitors see the text. Hidden text is identified as search spam by each of the major search engines.

Can I hide text in HTML to get a top ranking?

The simple and direct answer to the second part of the question is that you should not use hidden text. You may be able to trick the search engines for a brief period of time by hiding keyword stuffed sentences on your page, but you will risk having your site permanently banned from the search engines. As Google states on their SEO Services page, "search engine optimization is not a process of manipulating or tricking the search engines."

Below we will describe in detail the methods that misinformed webmasters and search engine optimization beginners often use to create invisible or hidden text in Web pages. The method worked wonders back in the mid 90's, before search engines were able to automatically filter the pages better.

It was a time when search engines were eager to index as many pages as possible - to grow their empires. Back then, much spam was tolerated. Google founders specifically referred to the manipulation of search results as a factor that compelled them to create Google.

In a Stanford paper titled **The Anatomy of a Large-Scale Hyper textual Web Search Engine by Sergey Brin and Lawrence Page**, Brin and Page state that their first design goal is to improve search quality and later state that "any text on the page which is not directly represented to the user is abused to manipulate search engines."|

Hidden Text & Google's Terms of Service

Google has some very clearly stated opinions about the use of hidden text.

From: Google Information for Webmasters - Webmaster Guidelines

"Quality Guidelines - Specific Recommendations: Avoid hidden text or hidden links."

From: Google - Report a Spam Report

"Trying to deceive (spam) our web crawler by means of hidden text, deceptive cloaking or doorway pages compromises the quality of our results and degrades the search experience for everyone. We think that's a bad thing."

Yahoo! now has its own search engine and has a very clear policy on hidden text.

From: Yahoo! Help > Search Help > Search Spam & Deletions > What is search engine spam?

"Search engine spam is pages that are considered unwanted and appear in search results with the intent to deceive or attract clicks at the expense of a poor user experience."

DOORWAY PAGES

If a visitor clicks through to a typical doorway page from a search engine results page, in most cases they will be redirected with a fast Meta refresh command to another page. Other forms of redirection include use of JavaScript and server side redirection, either through the .htaccess file or from the server configuration file. Some doorway pages may be dynamic pages generated by scripting languages such as Perl and PHP.

Doorway pages are often easy to identify in that they have been designed primarily for search engines, not for human beings. Sometimes a doorway page is copied from another high ranking page, but this is likely to cause the search engine to detect the page as a duplicate and exclude it from the search engine listings.

Because many search engines give a penalty for using the META refresh command, some doorway pages just trick the visitor into clicking on a link to get them to the desired destination page, or they use JavaScript for redirection. Bad, bad, bad.

Landing pages are regularly compared to equate to Doorway pages within the SEO literature and should be avoided. The former are content rich pages to which traffic is directed to within the context of pay-per-click campaigns and to maximize SEO campaigns.

Redirects

Redirecting a web page or site to another site can risky, as you could lose organic rankings and PR value you've spent so long building up.

There are some best methods of going about it though, if you need to. And sometimes you need to redirect an old page to a new page, or an old site to a new site.

301 Redirect

301 redirect is the most efficient and Search Engine Friendly method for webpage redirection. It's not hard to implement and it should preserve your search engine rankings for that particular page. If you have to change file names or move pages around, it's the safest option. The code "301" is interpreted as "moved permanently".

You can Test your redirection with a Search Engine Friendly Redirect Checker. Google for one.

Below are a Couple of methods to implement URL Redirection

IIS Redirect

- In internet services manager, right click on the file or folder you wish to redirect

- Select the radio titled "a redirection to a URL".

- Enter the redirection page

- Check "The exact URL entered above" and the "A permanent redirection for this resource"

- Click on 'Apply'

ColdFusion Redirect

```
<.cfheader statuscode="301" statustext="Moved permanently">
<.cfheader name="Location" value="http://www.new-url.com">
```

PHP Redirect

```
<?
Header( "HTTP/1.1 301 Moved Permanently" );
Header( "Location: http://www.new-url.com" );
?>
```

ASP Redirect

```
<%@ Language=VBScript %>
<%
Response.Status="301 Moved Permanently"
Response.AddHeader "Location","http://www.new-url.com/"
%>
```

ASP .NET Redirect

```
<script runat="server">
private void Page Load(object sender, System.EventArgs e)
{
Response.Status = "301 Moved Permanently";
Response.AddHeader("Location","http://www.new-url.com");
}
</script>
```

JSP (Java) Redirect

```
<%
response.setStatus(301);
response.setHeader( "Location", "http://www.new-url.com/" );
response.setHeader( "Connection", "close" );
%>
```

CGI PERL Redirect

```
$q = new CGI;
print $q->redirect("http://www.new-url.com/");
```

Ruby on Rails Redirect

```
def old_action
headers["Status"] = "301 Moved Permanently"
redirect_to "http://www.new-url.com/"
end
```

Redirect Old domain to New domain (htaccess redirect)

Create a .htaccess file with the below code, it will ensure that all your directories and pages of your old domain will get correctly redirected to your new domain. The .htaccess file needs to be placed in the root directory of your old website (i.e. the same directory where your index file is placed).

```
Options +FollowSymLinks
RewriteEngine on
RewriteRule (.*) http://www.newdomain.com/$1 [R=301,L]
```

Replace www.newdomain.com in the above code with your actual domain name.

Note* This .htaccess method of redirection works only on Linux servers having the Apache Mod-Rewrite moduled enabled.

How to Redirect HTML

Please refer to section titled 'How to Redirect with htaccess',

Off topic keywords

Don't use words on your website or in your source code, meta tags that don't relate to your website. SEO is theme based.

Cloaking

Cloaking is a black hat search engine optimization (SEO) technique in which the content presented to the search engine spider is different to that presented to the user. This is done by delivering content based on the IP addresses or the User-Agent HTTP header of the user requesting the website page.

When a user is identified as a search engine spider, a server-side script delivers a different version of the web page, one that contains content not present on the visible page.

The purpose of cloaking is to deceive search engines so they display the page when it would not otherwise be displayed.

Cloaking is often used as a spam technique, to try to trick search engines into giving the relevant site a higher ranking; it can also be used to trick search engine users into visiting a site based on the search engine description which site turns out to have substantially different, or even pornographic content. This is why search engines discount cloaking.

Cloaking is a form of the doorway page technique.

Hidden links

Hiding links in the background of a page by making it the same color as the background is bad. It may or may not be detected, depending on how many links there are, but it is a gamble, and considered "black hat" SEO – or evil SEO practices.

Chapter 8:
Social Media: SMM, SMO
(social media marketing, social media optimization)

Social media marketing/SMM and social media optimization is the art/science of getting online traffic from social sources on the internet.

The most popular social platforms you may recognize would be Facebook, Twitter, Instagram, Google Plus, LinkedIn, WP Blogs, Pinterest, YouTube.

Using social media marketing to tie together with an organic SEO and pay per click marketing campaign, is what many businesses do to gain success online.

YOU CAN DO THE SAME! (or hire someone)

It takes a lot of time. But if you are disciplined and can do 1 hour a day it will yield results. Or you can HIRE someone to do all the work. There are plenty of intermediate SEO's, especially in their 20's and 30's who are on the edge of technology and have the energy to type like a wild fire to accomplish your social media marketing. Elance.com or similar freelance sites are great for finding affordable talented web programmers around the world.

SO WHAT CAN <u>YOU</u> DO IF YOU KNOW THE INTERNET?

Content marketing

Post photos on Flickr, Facebook, Instagram, create blogs and write every day, make a Google+ account and tie it into your blogs and websites.

Get new friends on social network sites, create new blogs and new web pages, update your content, and link your content together in a web. Share posts. Write comments. **PARTICIPATE!**

Post comments on blogs and forums linking back to your website. Gain friends on Facebook and LinkedIn that are consumers or partners. Optimize your social media pages by filling them with text and image and video content, and links to your websites.

Post info about a new product on Twitter. Tweet away, if it works for your business. *Many small businesses don't get much benefit from Twitter—besides athletes, actors, big brands, musicians, politicians, etc.*

Get involved with social bookmark sites like Reddit and Digg.

Work on press releases and send them out quarterly. Prweb.com is a great system for small-medium businesses.

Create articles on your theme and submit them to article directories. Free and paid article sites are available on the net.

Blogs

What is a blog? It sounds creepy and rubbery. And there's about 200 million of them on the internet.

A blog is simply an online diary indexed in search engines like web pages, and with the advent of social media, sharing, etc… can be leveraged to gain online traffic and brand awareness along with your website(s), and listings and social platforms.

Content marketing includes press releases, blogs, and Internet marketing such as image marketing, shopping and video marketing.

A blog is a web site, maintained by its author with commentary, descriptions of events, or other material such as images or video. "Blog" can also be used as a verb, meaning to maintain or add content to a blog.

Years ago, a blog was not known as a good method of online marketing. Work from home blogs and stay at home mom blogs didn't appeal to businesses.

But now they do, as the search engines mix results together for a search, and blog results appear alongside other results. So now, many businesses are taking advantage of content marketing and blogging daily, weekly, monthly and seeing results!

The ability for readers to leave comments in an interactive format is an important part of many blogs and social media. Most blogs are primarily textual, although some focus videos (vlog), music

(MP3 blog), audio (podcasting), which are part of a wider network of social media.

Blog Types

Personal Blogs
>The personal blog, an ongoing diary or commentary by an individual, is the most widely used blog. But there are many ways to make a blog work for your business.

But business blogging is a reliable form of traffic using:

Corporate Blogs
Question Blogging
By Media Type
By Device
By Genre

Starting a blog

To start a blog, you have to select a blog host and a blogging software so you can write and upload your blog to the World Wide Web.

I suggest Google's free BlogSpot, and WordPress for their ability to rank well, but there are many free and paid blogging options out there. You can even integrate a blog on your business website, which is becoming more and more popular.

Blog hosts and blogging programs are available at various monthly costs or for free.

Blogs can be so easy, a non-tech savvy individual can manage and post a blog every day through a control panel. No programming skills required.

10 Ways To Optimize Your Blog

1. Tags: create keyword tags on your posts

2. Add a "Related Posts" feature

3. Include a call to action and include a form mail script for leads

4. Add "next" and "previous" post buttons

5. Build inbound links

6. Utilize titles and meta tags on posts

7. Register your blog at Technorati and use Technorati tags. Use Digg. Reddit. Social media bookmarks.

8. Make sure your BRAND is visible

9. Use keyword tools to find out which bloggers are most influential in conversations going on.

10. Get into other bloggers' blog rolls

Pinging your blog (no, it's not sexual)

In the blogging world, ping is an XML-RPC-based push mechanism by which a weblog notifies a server that its content has been updated. An XML-RPC signal is sent to one or more "ping servers," which generate blogs that have new material. Many blog authoring tools automatically ping one or more servers each time the blogger creates a new post or updates a post on the blog.

VIDEO OPTIMIZATION

Videos appear on organic results. So they are a viable form of content marketing. I suggest using You Tube videos, as the platform is easy to manage and it's owned by Google, so of course You Tube results are important to Google SEO.

To optimize a video, ensure you include a title and description with keywords and a link to your site or blog. Within the system you can monitor your viewer stats with You Tube's analytics.

To market videos, you can embed them on your websites and blogs, or in press releases, on Facebook, get votes for your videos, and create links pointing to your You Tube video page. Optimize your user profile with keywords.

Note: do NOT put affiliate marketing links within your You Tube pages, as this is a violation, and your video will be deleted when the system discovers the links.

NOW MIX IT UP (and shake that thing)

So, if you are new at this, and learning, you can see it takes a variety of avenues to direct traffic to a site or multiple platforms for lead-flow and sales in the online market—which, face it, is the new world's marketplace.

Create and send a variety of content into the web, and traffic will boomerang back.

Do it incorrectly, and nothing will happen, or your websites can be removed from the internet.

Social media factors have become increasingly a vital factor in search engine criteria, as it incorporates participation which can be measured and weighed.

UTILIZING (GOOGLE) ANALYTICS

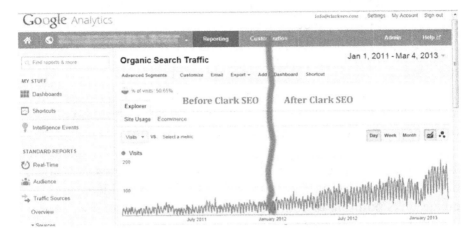

Ultimately, the goal of online marketing is to increase traffic. To do that in detail, a business should monitor their success, and they can easily. There are many analytics programs to track and analyze your website visitor data, but Google Analytics is one of the easiest, and it's free.

SIGN UP HERE: *www.google.com/analytics*

You are allowed 25 websites per email for free. You simply follow the instructions, and you will receive a script code to insert in the <head> section of your website or blogs. The <head> section contains your title, meta tags and other unseen code.

Note: *until recently, Google allowed the Analytics code anywhere before </body>. When they updated the system, all code must be moved to the head section to function and pull data. So if you have not updated your Google Analytics prior to 2013, your tracking code may be in the body section, and not able to pull data.*

Google Analytics allows you to see and track visitors by a variety of ways including geography, time spent on site, pages visited, keyword used to come to site, sources of traffic, conversions for pay per click, and much more.

JUST DO IT (and do it over and over again)

Just do something, every day, or have someone within your business do something every day, or hire a SEO to do a monthly program. A seasoned pro can accomplish in one hour what an intermediate could never accomplish in 100 hours.

It takes time. But online marketing, like your business, builds momentum. Once the ball rolls, it rolls hard and heavy, fast and beautiful – opening the gates of traffic to your wonderful service or product based website or platform landing pages, where you capture information for sales.

Online marketing is a new form for a new era. If businesses fail to adapt, learn and implement online strategies, they will suffer a disadvantage in the marketplace.

Start early. Build momentum. Gain rankings from diverse content. Smash your online competition.

Stay in tune with search engine updates.

Win the game in the new world marketplace.

Glossary

CPC: AdWords or pay per click system term meaning cost per click.

DMOZ: Google's human edited directory.

Google AdWords: Google's pay per click system in which you bid for clicks on their search engine and network sites.

Keywords: targeted themes and words your customers search with.

ROI: Return on investment.

Search engine optimization: aka SEO.

SEO aka **Search Engine Optimization** (one of the most used) is the technique which helps search engines to find and get better positioning for your website on top of millions of other sites competing. SEO, helps search engines to better understand the content of your website and therefore helps you get more traffic.

Search Engine Results Page (SERP)

SERP or **Search Engine Results Page** is simply the result page that shows the search engine. When you enter a keyword or a set of keywords the search engine display a list of websites. Using this list we can optimize our website for better positioning.

SEM or **Search Engine Marketing** is the process of gaining traffic or visibility in the search engines. Often abbreviated as "search marketing". **SEM** also includes two basic areas: Gain traffic through SEO efforts. **SEA** (**Search Engine Advertising**) – Earn traffic through paid advertising, such as Google AdWords. **Social Media Optimization (SMO)**

SERM or **Search Engine Reputation Management** simply tries to control your website reputation when a user performs a search. If there are negative comments about your website the SERM will try to use these techniques to avoid appearing before the positive.

SMO stands for **Social Media Optimization** and includes all processes to increase the visibility of a website in social networks (Facebook, Twitter, LinkedIn, Google+ YouTube etc.) increasing the links pointing to your website, and therefore increasing SERP positioning.

SMM or *Social Media Marketing* is used to promote a website through all sorts of social media, for example, include a link to a content that can reach thousands of users within social network. The main objective is to generate brand and visibility in the search engine.

INDEX

Internet Bibliography

Brin, S. and Page, L. (1998)
The Anatomy of a Large-Scale Hypertextual Web Search:
Enginehttp://infolab.stanford.edu/~backrub/google.html

Search Engine Round Table (as of July 2014)
http://www.seroundtable.com/

Wikipedia (as of July 2014)
http://en.wikipedia.org/wiki/Search_engine_optimization

www.ingramcontent.com/pod-product-compliance
Lightning Source LLC
Chambersburg PA
CBHW061031050326
40689CB00012B/2764